CIP LOW

Compliance Program Guide

Building a successful compliance program for
Low Impact BES Cyber Systems

Terry Schurter
Karl Perman
Marc Grayson

ISBN: 978-0-9972522-4-8

Cover design by Tugboat Design

This book is focused on protecting Low Impact only BES assets, and their associated BES Cyber Systems & Cyber Assets.

Based on NERC CIP Standards CIP-002-5.1a and CIP-003-6, with relevant consideration for pending versions CIP-003-7 and CIP-003-TCA, the steps and actions needed to ensure NERC CIP compliance are laid out here in plain English.

So whether you need a refresher, are filling an information gap, prepping for upcoming compliance dates, or just like to read as much as you can about such an enthralling subject like NERC CIP Compliance, we think you'll find something value in these pages.

The goal of this book is to see through the trees to find the forest because the better we understand what we are doing, the better we will be at doing it.

Also by Karl Perman and Terry Schurter,
for Medium and High Impact BES Cyber Systems:

PROTECTING CRITICAL INFRASTRUCTURE

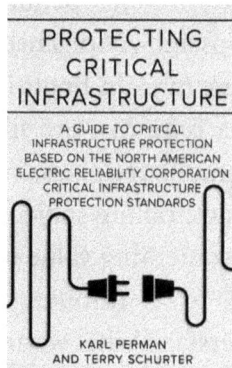

Available at:
Print: http://www.amazon.com/
Protecting-Critical-Infrastructure-Reliability-Corporation/dp/0997252227
eBook: https://ganxy.com/i/112294

Foreword

The North American Electric Reliability Corporation (NERC) has developed a set of Compliance Standards related to critical infrastructure protection (CIP) for electric generation and transmission entities.

The NERC CIP Version 6 Standards are more demanding and comprehensive than the preceding CIP Version 3 Standards. CIP Version 6 brings a substantial number of assets under NERC CIP for the first time, many under the Low Impact Requirements of the Standards.

While Low Impact Requirements are less rigorous than those for Medium or High Impact, effort, preparation and more importantly sustainment is required to ensure compliance and reliability.

This book details the evidence that must be collected, the Lists that must be managed, the documents that must be controlled, and the oversight that must be implemented to ensure compliance in accordance with the low impact requirements in the NERC CIP Standards.

Consider it your "cheat sheet" to CIP Low compliance. Use it well!

Sincerely,
Terry Schurter, Karl Perman, and Marc Grayson

CIP Core, Inc.

Terry Schurter, Karl Perman, and Marc Grayson (the authors of this book) are also the founders, of CIP Core, Inc.

CIP Core is a nonprofit corporation whose mission is to: *deliver educational materials and services, including but not limited to, online training, educational resources, and other resources, to the electric industry in North America for the purposes of improving and protecting the reliability of the Bulk Electric System.*

CIP Core has training courses on NERC CIP and Cyber Security that are designed for general audiences. CIP Core provides these courses and other educational resources to the industry in a subscription model, with all training courses available as SCORM 1.2 packages and as MP4s with exercise scripts.

To learn more about CIP Core, please visit:
www.CIPCore.org

Contents

CIP Version 6 and CIP Low

In CIP version 3, regulated entities assessed their BES (Bulk Electric System) assets against an internal risk-based assessment methodology to determine if they were critical or not. If the answer was "not" then the entity had no further compliance responsibilities of any significance under NERC CIP.

That has changed under CIP Version 6. Now entities must perform their BES asset assessments (system identification and classification) using a *bright-line* set of criteria to determine the BES Cyber Systems and the Impact Rating of the BES Cyber Systems.

There are some important concepts that can help simplify what is really happening here. With all of the terms and compliance language getting thrown around, it's easy to get confused about how things really come together.

The first concept is a BES asset. A BES asset is the "facility, site, or system" that serves one or more of the functions of the asset types included in the Standards. NERC uses BES asset as an informal term, which is why the "a" in "asset" is not capitalized in the NERC CIP Standards.

So the next question becomes, what are the BES asset types?

NERC CIP Version 6 provides the answer in the assessment criteria in the CIP-002.5.1a Standard. BES assets are:

1) Control Centers and Backup Control Centers
2) Substations and Switchyards
3) Generation Facilities
4) System Restoration and Protection Systems

These are the functional categories of the components of the Bulk Electric System that are protected under the NERC CIP Standards.

Many BES assets are physically easy to identify. We can point a finger at these BES assets and say, "that power plant is there" or "this substation is here." They have a unique physical location and a prominent physical form. Even a layperson can identify a coal-fired power plant and the substations they drive by frequently in their life.

The identification of BES assets helps to clarify what unique facilities, systems, and equipment comprise our power system. Knowing what BES assets we have and the functions they perform helps us define risk-based approaches to CIP compliance, physical and cyber security in an effective manner.

The second important concept is that the NERC CIP Standards are designed to protect BES assets *by protecting their associated BES Cyber Systems and Cyber Assets* because of their importance in operating BES assets and their vulnerability to being attacked. They are microprocessors and face all of the threats any other computer systems face.

This means that in order to protect our BES assets, we must protect their constituent BES Cyber Systems and Cyber Assets. We are still protecting the BES asset, but we are doing quite a bit to shore-up our weakest link: *all those systems we rely on to operate our assets.*

The third important concept is that Low Impact Requirements are focused specifically on BES assets and not BES Cyber Systems or Cyber Assets. To be compliant under NERC CIP with Low Impact only does *not require* documenting BES Cyber Systems or BES Cyber Assets.

This has been a point of confusion for many. Under the NERC CIP-003-6 Standard there are the terms LERC (Low Impact Electronic Connectivity) and LEAP (Low Impact Electronic Access Point) that blur the lines and seem to suggest the need to document some BES Cyber Assets.

There is another way to look at this, though. For example, a firewall could act as a LEAP for a network or network segment. A network diagram that demonstrates the BES Cyber Assets on the network are protected by a Firewall is one way to demonstrate that all LERC is protected by a LEAP.

This seems to make sense when looking at CIP-003-7 and CIP-003-TCA (Transient Cyber Assets), both of which address mandates from FERC, we can see that NERC has addressed this issue and resolved the confusion:

Rationale for Requirement R2:

In response to FERC Order No. 791, Requirement R2 requires entities to develop and implement cyber security plans to meet specific security control objectives for assets containing low impact BES Cyber System(s). The cyber security plan(s) covers four subject matter areas: (1) cyber security awareness; (2) physical security controls; (3) electronic access controls; and (4) Cyber Security Incident response. This plan(s), along with the cyber security policies required under Requirement R1, Part 1.2, provides a framework for operational, procedural, and technical safeguards for low impact BES Cyber Systems.

Considering the varied types of low impact BES Cyber Systems across the BES, Attachment 1 provides Responsible Entities flexibility on how to apply the security controls to meet the security objectives. Additionally, because many Responsible Entities have multiple-impact rated BES Cyber Systems, nothing in the requirement prohibits entities from using their high and medium impact BES Cyber System policies, procedures, and processes to implement security controls required for low impact BES Cyber Systems, as detailed in Requirement R2, Attachment 1.

Responsible Entities will use their identified assets containing low impact BES Cyber System(s) (developed pursuant to CIP-002) to substantiate the sites or locations associated with low impact BES Cyber System(s). However, there is no requirement or compliance expectation for Responsible Entities to maintain a list(s) of individual low impact BES Cyber System(s) and their associated cyber assets or to maintain a list of authorized users.

Source: North American Electric Reliability Corporation (NERC)

In CIP-002-5.1a Appendix 1 a discrete list of BES Cyber Systems is specifically not required, further reinforcing the lack of a compliance requirement to maintain such a list.

Appendix 1

Requirement Number and Text of Requirement

CIP-002-5.1, Requirement R1

R1. Each Responsible Entity shall implement a process that considers each of the following assets for purposes of parts 1.1 through 1.3:

    i. Control Centers and backup Control Centers;

    ii. Transmission stations and substations;

    iii. Generation resources;

    iv. Systems and facilities critical to system restoration, including Blackstart Resources and Cranking Paths and initial switching requirements;

    v. Special Protection Systems that support the reliable operation of the Bulk Electric System; and

    vi. For Distribution Providers, Protection Systems specified in Applicability section 4.2.1 above.

1.1. Identify each of the high impact BES Cyber Systems according to Attachment 1, Section 1, if any, at each asset;

1.2. Identify each of the medium impact BES Cyber Systems according to Attachment 1, Section 2, if any, at each asset; and

1.3. Identify each asset that contains a low impact BES Cyber System according to Attachment 1, Section 3, if any (a discrete list of low impact BES Cyber Systems is not required).

Source: North American Electric Reliability Corporation (NERC)

So it seems consistent, and well supported, that the only list that is required for NERC CIP Low Impact only compliance is a list of Low Impact BES Assets. There are no compliance expectations to maintain any lists of low impact BES Cyber Systems and their associated Cyber Assets, though there is certainly nothing prohibiting maintaining these lists either. This Low Impact Only BES Asset list would, therefore, be generated and managed as part of the Low Impact BES Asset Assessment Process.

Hopefully these concepts will help in developing a clear understanding of the security and compliance expectations for NERC CIP BES assets with Low Impact only BES Cyber Systems. Let's go through them one more time.

1) A BES asset is a site, facility or system performing one or more of the functions of:
    a. Control Centers and Backup Control Centers
    b. Substations and Switchyards
    c. Generation Facilities
    d. System Restoration and Protection Systems
2) NERC CIP is designed to protect BES assets
    a. (only High and Medium Impact require extensive BES Cyber System and Cyber Asset protection)
3) Low Impact is focused specifically on BES assets, not BES Cyber Systems or Cyber Assets

Requirements, Sub-Requirements - now Sections

The NERC Standards are devised as a set of Standards with a number of Requirements, like CIP-003-6 (the Standard): R1 (the Requirement, number 1). It is common practice for NERC Standards to also have sub-requirements several levels deep like R1.1 and R1.1.1.

CIP-003-6 includes an appendix with Sections that provide detail on the Requirements for Low Impact BES assets. Sections can have their own sub-requirements resulting in a hierarchy like CIP-003-6: R2 Section 3.1. These Sections work just like any other compliance requirement where their rules must be followed and evidence gathered in order to demonstrate compliance.

Now before we dig into the requirements themselves, let's make sure we understand the importance of Compliance Evidence and Compliance Controls.

Compliance Evidence and Controls

In order to demonstrate compliance with the NERC CIP Standards regulated entities must understand the concept of performance-based compliance. That means regulated entities are expected to be able to show tangible evidence they have followed all Requirements at all times.

For example, if a policy needs to be reviewed every 15 months, then the entity should have documentation that shows the review was indeed performed. The entity's documentation should include the details of what was done and by whom each time the review was performed and historical records should demonstrate that the review was performed in each 15-month period it was required.

A NERC CIP regional audit can include historical evidence review that can span a number of years, so the Low Impact compliance program needs to collect and manage both current state and historical evidence. This needs to be built into to the foundation of the compliance program.

As part of the overall evidence management strategy, it's necessary to understand the types of evidence needed for each Requirement. From there a program can be built to manage and control compliance for Low Impact NERC CIP compliance. The evidence can be generalized into the following categories:

1. Controlled Documents
2. Process Artifacts
3. Data-Driven Reports
4. Collected Documents

Controlled Documents

Controlled documents are often referred to as living documents, meaning they are reviewed and revised on a periodic basis. Written policies and procedures are examples of living documents.

Version history must be maintained for controlled documents. There must also be a formal review process or procedure that is used to perform the review, and reviews must be completed per any mandatory schedule requirements.

Process Artifacts

Process artifacts demonstrate the operations of the process or procedure used to complete a compliance activity. This includes any checks performed, changes required, and approvals collected. It also includes who did each task in the process and when they completed it.

Data-Driven Reports

One of the areas that has been particularly challenging in implementing a successful NERC CIP compliance program are the things or resources that fall under NERC CIP. Here are a few examples:

1) BES Assets
2) BES Cyber Systems
3) Cyber Assets
4) People
5) Physical Access Rights
6) Electronic Access Rights

When we deal with these lists of things, the evidence needed to demonstrate compliance with NERC CIP is likely to include one or more reports generated from the data from one of these resources.

For Low Impact, the only list of things (we'll just call then a list from this point on) that is required is the BES asset list. In this book, we will outline the data that needs to be collected and where reports are likely to be used for evidence.

Golden Egg – the only list required is a Low Impact BES asset list. A list of discrete BES Cyber Systems is not required, just a list of BES sites, facilities or systems not classified as High or Medium Impact

We will cover the evidence that is likely to be required to demonstrate compliance for each Low Impact Requirement.

Collected Documents

The last type of evidence is collected documents. These can be any type of document that is collected either by manual or automated means that further demonstrates compliance with one or more NERC CIP Requirements.

For example, collected documents that demonstrate the process the entity went through when performing their BES asset assessment would likely be included with the BES asset list report. These documents might include meeting notes, completed forms, a formal analysis, or a 3rd party assessment.

Compliance Controls

Controls are what brings everything together. Even if multiple people and/or tools are involved, the Control for each Requirement must include all of the followings functions:

1) Mandatory Controls
   a. Scheduling and Schedule Monitoring
   b. Processes and/or Procedures
   c. Job Roles and Task Assignments
   d. Evidence Collection and Storage
   e. Evidence Generation
   f. Document Management

2) Optional Controls
    a. Compliance Checklists
    b. Approval Chains

Mandatory controls are those required to meet compliance, in this case, NERC CIP compliance. Optional controls are not required but can be used to increase compliance assurance.

Checklists are included, where applicable, as part of the task documentation where they apply. Checklists are typically questions that need to be signed-off before completing a review or approval. The task is already there to address the compliance requirement so the Checklist doubles-down on compliance assurance by explicitly requiring the reviewer to indicate compliance needs are met.

Approval chains rely more on external oversight, typically having two or three approval levels on compliance items. The idea here is to build a chain of accountability, with comprehensive oversight, behind all compliance activities.

The most important thing is to recognize the importance of controls for NERC CIP compliance and to ensure your strategy meets the minimum required to be in a state of compliance.

In this book, we will document these controls for each Low Impact Requirement.

Low Impact Implementation

Each topic covered in this book must be addressed to be CIP Low Impact compliant. The topics are presented in an order (chapters) that is roughly aligned to implementation order. But it's not that simple, so here are the details about the process of preparing for Low Impact compliance.

There are some dependencies in the requirements along with a good deal of flexibility. It all starts with getting leadership in place and performing the BES Asset Assessment.

Getting leadership in place requires that the entity has designated a CIP Senior Manager and documented that designation. The CIP Senior Manager must approve and sign-off on the BES Asset Assessment, so the CIP Senior Manager must be in place before all compliance requirements for the BES Asset Assessment can be met. The responsibilities of the CIP Senior Manager can also be delegated to others through a delegation process, and if delegates are used, all delegates and their delegations must be documented.

Drafting the entity's Cyber Security Policy can also start at any time, but like the BES Asset Assessment, it requires approval and sign-off by the CIP Senior Manager. There can also be results from the BES Asset Assessment that could play into the content included in the Cyber Security Policy, in which case it would not be completed prior to the completion of the BES Asset Assessment.

The remaining requirements logically start after the Cyber Security Policy is completed and approved because they must enforce the portion of the Cyber Security Policy that applies to them.

For example, if the Cyber Security Policy mandates the use of electronic locks with personal identification codes or scan cards on all protected physical assets then the Physical Access Controls evidence needs to demonstrate that type of physical security is actually in place.

The remaining requirements include physical and electronic access controls, security awareness, and incident response.

When it comes to building a compliance program, make sure to think about it as a holistic program. The Cyber Security Policy describes what the organization will do, the compliance program enforces, and the evidence that is generated and collected proves it.

1 – CIP Senior Manager

The NERC Standard CIP-003-6 Requirement 3 requires registered entities to designate a single senior management official as the entity's CIP Senior Manager.

The CIP Senior Manager has specific responsibilities, including approving specific aspects of the entity's CIP program including its Cyber Security Policy and BES Asset Assessment.

To complete the BES Asset Assessment and maintain ongoing compliance, the following actions will need to be taken.

Note – It is a Requirement that the CIP Senior Manager sign-off on specific compliance items, like the entity's BES Asset Assessment and Cyber Security Policy. Demonstrating this compliance can be done by printing the document, signing it, and then scanning it. One or more forms of digital signatures can also be used as long as the entity's Cyber Security Policy allows it.

Task 1 – Identify the new CIP Senior Manager

When designating the CIP Senior Manager, certain information needs to be gathered and recorded about each such designation. The information that needs to be collected is form-based data.

The form for the new CIP Senior Manager needs to include certain details that identify the CIP Senior Manager and provide the means to contact him or her. This includes his or her first name, last name, title, phone number, and email at a minimum. There should also be a date indicating when the designation became (or becomes) effective.

It's important to note that there is only one CIP Senior Manager so if the CIP Senior Manager is changed at any point, the entity's compliance evidence should clearly indicate the effective dates for each CIP Senior Manager, and demonstrate that no overlap exists (nor are there any gaps!)

Task 2 – Approve the New CIP Senior Manager

Once the form is completed, it needs to be reviewed and approved by someone with the authority to attest to this designation for the entity.

Task 3 – Generate a process artifact

The process artifact demonstrates the process the entity used to perform the new CIP Senior Manager designation. It should show that the proper information about the new CIP Senior Manager was collected, the information was reviewed and approved by a person with the appropriate approval authority, and the effective date has been documented, does not overlap, and does not leave a gap.

CIP Senior Manager Designation Controls

The Controls that must be applied to CIP Senior Manager Designation include:

Control – Require Initial Designation
It is required that an initial designation be performed. There are other Requirements that cannot be met without first meeting this Requirement.

Control – Perform the process for a New CIP Senior Manager
There is no requirement for a periodic review of the CIP Senior Manager. However, at any time that the CIP Senior Manager changes,

those changes must be documented and the appropriate evidence produced.

Note – Delegations of Authority must also be controlled, however, we discuss them as their own chapter rather than as a Control function here.

---

2 – BES Asset Assessment

NERC Standard CIP-002-5.1, Requirement 1.2 requires registered entities to perform and document the assessment of their BES assets.

To complete the BES Asset Assessment and maintain it in a state of compliance, the following actions will need to be taken.

Task 1 – Perform the BES Asset Assessment

Each regulated must perform a BES asset assessment using the criteria provided in the NERC Standards. This assessment may involve a number of people from different departments in your organization, personnel from other neighboring registered entities and organizations that perform reliability functions associated with your organization.

Regardless of how the process works out for each entity, it is recommended each entity document the process used to evaluate BES Assets for their criticality or impact-rating under CIP-002-5.1. From an audit perspective, this assists entities in explaining how the standard is applied and situations where unique engineering rationale is applied.

Assessment documentation is an important part of evidence, along with process and system (one-line diagrams) used at the time of the assessment and other supporting documentation.

Task 2 – Produce the Low Impact BES Asset List

BES asset data is best managed as a list because there are BES asset characteristics that must be documented for each BES asset. This will help produce the evidence needed to meet this Requirement and to help satisfy other related Requirements.

Note – the specific data likely to be needed to demonstrate compliance is presented in the chapter that covers its related Requirement. In this chapter, we include the data likely to be needed to demonstrate compliance with CIP-002-5.1 only.

Some of the data we need to collect is obvious. For example, we need some kind of unique identifier for each BES asset. That could be the name commonly used for the BES asset, like the name of a transmission station or generation resource or some other form of identifier the entity decides to use.

Because compliance evidence should be maintained for all of the time each BES asset is active[1], BES asset commissioned dates and decommissioned dates should be tracked.

The BES asset type, as defined in the NERC CIP Standards, should be recorded as part of each BES asset record in the list.

Even for BES assets with Low Impact BES Cyber Systems, the BES asset list should explicitly require the status for High, Medium and Low BCS to avoid any possibility of ambiguity.

CIP-003-6 includes the terms LERC and LEAP. These terms, however, are slated for retirement in the pending new versions (CIP-003-7, CIP-003-TCA) which is confusing at a glance, yet the same essential concepts are incorporated in the new versions which ultimately ensures Electronic Access Controls, such as a segmented, network perimeter around Cyber Assets within Low-Impact facilities, sites, and systems, are implemented.

---

1 Compliance evidence is not required for the time prior to the effective date of each NERC CIP Compliance Standard.

Standard Development Timeline

This section is maintained by the drafting team during the development of the standard and will be removed when the standard becomes effective.

Description of Current Draft

This draft of CIP-003-7 is addressing the directive issued by the Federal Energy Regulatory

Commission (Commission) in paragraph 73 of Order No. 822 which reads:

> [T]he Commission concludes that a modification to the Low Impact External Routable Connectivity definition to reflect the commentary in the Guidelines and Technical Basis section of CIP-003-6 is necessary to provide needed clarity to the definition and eliminate ambiguity surrounding the term "direct" as it is used in the proposed definition. Therefore, pursuant to section 215(d)(5) of the FPA, we direct NERC to develop a modification to provide the needed clarity, within one year of the effective date of this Final Rule approving revisions to the cybersecurity Critical Infrastructure Protection (CIP) standards.

In this revision, the SDT revised Sections 2 and 3 of Attachments 1 and 2 in CIP-003-7 and removed the terms *Low Impact External Routable Connectivity* (LERC) and *Low Impact BES Cyber System Electronic Access Point* (LEAP). The modifications incorporate concepts and select language from the LERC definition into Attachment 1, Section 3 and focus the requirement on implementing electronic access controls for asset(s) containing low impact BES Cyber System(s). The SDT simplified Section 3 of Attachment 1 to require the Responsible Entity to permit only necessary inbound and outbound electronic access when using a routable protocol entering or leaving the asset between low impact BES Cyber System(s) and a Cyber Asset(s) outside the asset containing low impact BES Cyber system(s).

Source: North American Electric Reliability Corporation (NERC)

As previously noted, the changes address a FERC mandate to clarify Low Impact criteria. The answer given by FERC is that CIP Low Impact is dealing with only BES assets themselves.

Note – because CIP-003-7 is likely to be approved, it is best to design the Low Impact compliance program to address both versions of the Standard. This is specific to Electronic Access Controls, as this is the primary section affected by the change. At this time, it is probably not necessary to include CIP-003-TCA in this plan, as its primary impact will be on Transient Devices, which will require new controls to be put into place.

Regardless of the version, when a BES asset has Low Impact Cyber Systems and/or Cyber Assets with low impact external routable connectivity and/or dial-up connectivity, this must be identified and documented. This information identifies the BES assets that are required to have electronic access controls on their Low Impact BES Cyber Systems and/or BES Cyber Assets.

Task 3 – Generate the BES asset List Report

Once the BES asset List has been produced, it is best to include a copy of the List as part of your evidence. That might also include:

- Running a report and saving it as a PDF
- Printing a copy of the List to a PDF using a PDF Printer
- Physically printing a copy, scanning it, and uploading it

Including a copy of the BES asset list with all characteristics documented addresses a number of key compliance objectives for this requirement.

Task 4 – Gather the CIP Senior Manager Sign-off

The CIP Senior Manager Sign-off is either an approved form of digital (as approved by the entity in its Cyber Security Policy) or wet-ink (scanned) signature. The signature needs to be on the documentation that details the BES asset assessment results and BES asset characteristics. The CIP Senior Manager is in effect, signing off on the data in the BES asset List and placing his or her stamp of approval on all other evidence.

This can be handled by signing specific pieces of evidence, such as the BES asset List report; signing off on a form created by the entity, or through a review and approval step in a workflow solution that produces a workflow report for the process.

Compliance Checklist

The optional compliance checklist items that may be considered for this task are:
1) BES Asset Impact Ratings Correct?
2) BES Asset assessment evidence complete?
3) Routable Communication and Dial-up Connectivity evidence complete?

Task 5 – Generate a process artifact

The process artifact demonstrates the process the entity used to perform the assessment and complete the review and approval. It should show who did what and when.

This evidence can be a created through the use of a single manual form, multiple forms, or a workflow solution. The main thing is to demonstrate that a formal process was followed when performing and approving the assessment, and that the appropriate people performed each Task. That along with dates that demonstrate when the work was performed provides the evidence needed to demonstrate successful execution of the entity's assessment process.

BES Asset Assessment Controls

The Controls that must be applied to BES asset assessment include:

Control – Require initial assessment
It is required that an initial assessment be performed. This should be completed first, along with the CIP Senior Manager designation.

Control – Perform the Review on a Scheduled Basis
The Cyber Security Policy must be reviewed (and updated if needed) at least once every 15 months.

Control – Perform the process on a BES asset change
The assessment process should be performed when anything changes in the BES asset List, the change (or changes) should go through the assessment process in order to generate the new effective BES asset List along with review and approval by the CIP Senior Manager. While BES assessment evidence may not be required for all changes, the rest of the evidence should be produced to document the changes to the BES asset List.

3 – Delegations of Authority

The NERC Standard CIP-003-6 Requirement 4 requires registered entities to document any Delegations of Authority granted by the CIP Senior Manager.

Delegations of Authority are used to authorize other personnel to act on behalf of the CIP Senior Manager when approving and signing-off on specific compliance items.

While it is not required that the CIP Senior Manager make any Delegations of Authority, it is required that when delegations are made, they are formally documented and approved.

Each authorization should explicitly include all NERC Standards and Requirements for which Authority has been delegated. This can include multiple delegations per person.

To maintain ongoing compliance with Delegations of Authority, the following actions will need to be taken.

Task 1 – Documenting Delegations of Authority

When documenting Delegations of Authority made by the CIP Senior Manager, certain information needs to be gathered and recorded about each such delegation. The information that needs to be collected is form-based data.

Note – it may be easier to manage Delegations of Authority through a form created in a desktop application like a word processor or spreadsheet application. If Delegations of Authority are maintained in this way, the primary purpose of Task 1 is to collect the updated Delegations of Authority document.

The form for the Delegations of Authority needs to include certain details that identify the person or persons being granted authority. This includes his or her first name, last name, title, phone number, and email at a minimum. There should also be a date indicating when the delegation became (or becomes) effective, and it may also include when a delegation expires (is no longer effective). Regardless of the specific fields used to document Delegations of Authority, it must always be clear what the current Delegations of Authority are including applicable standard, requirement and specific actions being delegated, and for compliance, it is also necessary to have the same information available historically.

It's important to note that there can be more than one person with the same delegated authority. There is no limitation on the number of Delegates a CIP Senior Manager can have or what authority each Delegate is given. This is up to the CIP Senior Manager and may include considerations like ensuring redundancy for CIP Senior Manager responsibilities and distributing authority to certain locations or operating units.

Note – because the CIP Senior Manager is the person responsible for making and approving all Delegations of Authority this can often be accomplished with a single Task.

Task 2 – Generate a process artifact

The process artifact demonstrates the process the entity used to perform all Delegations of Authority. It should show that the proper information about each Delegate was collected, including the authority granted for each, and be signed-off on by the CIP Senior Manager.

Delegations of Authority Controls

The Controls that must be applied to CIP Senior Manager Designation include:

Control – If they exist, initially Document Delegations of Authority

If Delegations of Authority are or have been made, they must be formally documented and approved (CIP Senior Manager sign-off).

Control – Perform the process for each change to Delegations of Authority

There is no requirement for a periodic review of Delegations of Authority. However, any time there is a change to the Delegations of Authority, those changes must be documented and the appropriate evidence produced within 30 days of the actual change.

4 – Cyber Security Policy

The NERC Standard CIP-003-6 Requirement R1 requires registered entities to have a formal Cyber Security Policy. The specific Requirements for Low Impact are under sub-section R1.2 and are described in detail in sub-sections R1.2.1 – R1.2.4.

The Cyber Security Policy is the overall security game plan for the entity and it must describe a cyber security strategy that clearly addresses the NERC CIP Requirements that apply to the entity.

The Cyber Security Policy must be reviewed on a periodic basis, no less than every fifteen (15) months. It is expected that each entity will seek to identify any improvements, adaptations, or adjustments that can further enhance the entity's overall Physical Cyber Security posture. This includes addressing new threats or threat vectors not previously considered in the plan (a key element in staying up with the ever-changing attack environment).

Note – while the Cyber Security Policy is referred to in singular in the NERC CIP Standards, it can actually be made up of multiple documents that in their totality make up the entity's Cyber Security Plan.

To achieve and maintain ongoing compliance, the following actions will need to be taken.

Task 1 – Review Cyber Security Policy

When performing the Cyber Security Policy Review, the reviewer is expected to assess each of the sections of the Cyber Security Policy

that address each of the following sub-sections (R1.2.1 – R1.2.4):
1) Cyber Security Awareness
2) Physical Security Controls
3) Electronic Access Controls
4) Cyber Security Incident Response

If changes to the Cyber Security Policy are required, the reviewer needs to document what needs to change and should provide as much information as possible to describe the change or the rationale behind it. This information will be used in the next step, where required changes are made.

If no changes are required, the review must indicate this so that the entity has the evidence required to demonstrate the Policy was reviewed and no changes were required.

Task 2 – Update Cyber Security Policy

If changes are required once the Cyber Security Policy review is complete, the required changes need to be reviewed and the Cyber Security Policy needs to be updated to address the concerns identified.

To do this, the person or persons responsible for updating the Cyber Security Policy need the information from the Cyber Security Policy reviewer. It is this information that tells those responsible for updating the plan what they need to address.

Task 1 (repeat)

When changes to the Cyber Security Plan need to be made, it's best to perform the first task (review Cyber Security Policy) again, once the changes are complete. In the ideal compliance and assurance process, the CIP Senior Manager will always receive the Cyber Security Policy directly after it has been reviewed and approved by the person or personnel assigned that responsibility.

Once the review is complete, if no additional changes are required, the updated Cyber Security Policy is ready for the CIP Senior Manager's review and approval.

Task 3 – CIP Senior Manager Approval

Once the Cyber Security Policy has been reviewed and approved, it must be signed-off by the CIP Senior Manager. This applies to both:
1) Approved - no changes required
2) Approved - changes implemented, & reviewed

For compliance, the approval for the CIP Senior Manager, the date of the approval and the signature of the CIP Senior Manager should be collected.

The CIP Senior Manager will need the information about the review, and any changes that were made, along with the Policy(s) themselves, for his or her review. Once the CIP Senior Manager approves the Cyber Security Policy all that is left is to generate the process artifact.

However, the CIP Senior Manager may not approve the Cyber Security Policy. When this is the case, the CIP Senior Manager should document the reasons why he or she is not approving the Policy and send it back to review (task 1).

Task 2 – Generate a process artifact

The process artifact demonstrates the process the entity used to review the Cyber Security Policy, identify any changes required, perform any required updating of the Policy, and gather the CIP Senior Manager approval.

It should show that Cyber Security Policy was reviewed within the required schedule of at least once every 15 months, that it was approved by the CIP Senior Manager, the CIP Senior Manager's signature and documentation of any changes that were made.

Cyber Security Policy Controls

The Controls that must be applied to the Cyber Security Policy include:

Control – Required initially

It is required to have a Cyber Security Policy in place that has been approved by the CIP Senior Manager.

Control – Perform the Review on a Scheduled Basis

The Cyber Security Policy must be reviewed (and updated if needed) at least once every 15 months.

Note – the Cyber Security Policy can be updated at any time, and there are cases where entities are likely to update their Policy to address a concern or lesson learned at the time they become aware of it. When this happens, it is best to perform a review and update in the formal manner described herein to ensure consistent process and generation/collection of evidence. This does reset the 15-month clock.

---

5 - Security Awareness

The NERC Standard CIP-003-6 Requirement R2 Section 1 requires registered entities to reinforce cyber security practices at least once every fifteen (15) calendar months with Security Awareness.

This is included for Low Impact BES assets because people are essential to critical infrastructure protection. When people know and understand their role in protecting critical infrastructure they become a powerful mechanism to reduce attack surfaces, detect anomalies, and respond to issues. Without that awareness, mistakes, often due to lax procedures and inadequate training, can directly expose the organization to cyber or physical attack.

Security awareness is used to educate people on the organization's security practices, and the importance of following them correctly. It is also used to sensitize personnel to the various types of threats. Common ways to deliver Security Awareness content include:

1) Direct Communications:
   a. Emails
   b. Memos
   c. Computer-based training
2) Indirect Communications:
   a. Posters
   b. Intranet posts and content
   c. Brochures and pamphlets

Multiple types of awareness activities are not required for compliance with Low Impact BES assets but using more than one activity type is likely to achieve a better result. Scheduling secure awareness activities on a regular basis, not just at the end of the schedule period, is another way to improve the overall security behavior of people.

To achieve and maintain ongoing compliance for Security Awareness, the following actions will need to be taken.

Task 1 – Perform Security Awareness Activities

Security Awareness activities need to be conducted and logged at least once every fifteen (15) months.

When security awareness activities are conducted, a copy of the Security Awareness material should be collected for evidence, along with when the Security Awareness activity was conducted, and the type of activity (i.e. – like the communication types listed above).

It is also beneficial to identify the scope of the Security Awareness activity in respect to the people it reaches, such as all personnel (posters, intranet postings, mass email) or a specific group of personnel (department email, meetings, etc.).

Each person that performs a Security Awareness activity should be responsible for logging their activity and including a copy of the Security Awareness content as evidence.

Task 2 – Review Security Awareness Activities

Reviewing Security Awareness activities is desirable to ensure all Security Awareness activities have been properly documented.

While the review is not mandatory (does not directly meet a compliance requirement), it is the best way to be certain the entity has performed mandatory Security Awareness activities and collected the appropriate evidence for same.

The review should assess the Security Awareness activities that have been completed to determine if they meet the NERC CIP requirements. The review should be done before the end of the mandatory 15-month cycle to ensure the entity has time to resolve any issues that may be uncovered.

Any issues that are identified should be documented so that they can be resolved. If no issues are identified, the Resolve Issues task is not required.

Compliance Checklist

The optional compliance checklist items that may be considered for this task are:

1) Completed Security Awareness activities meet compliance requirements?
2) Evidence Demonstrates Cyber Security Practices Reinforcement?

Task 3 – Resolve Issues

If the review uncovers any issues (i.e. – missing documentation, insufficient Security Awareness activities) the issues need to be resolved.

The person(s) resolving Security Awareness issues needs access to the Security Awareness activity documentation and the review information where issues are identified. All resolved issues should be documented, and when issue resolution is complete, the Security Awareness Activity Review should be conducted again (until it passes the Review).

Task 4 – Generate a process artifact

The process artifact for Security Awareness is primarily used for assessing the current state of compliance. It demonstrates that the entity reviewed its Security Awareness activities, and approved them, within the mandatory schedule.

However, the process artifact is not mandatory evidence, although it can be used as supplemental evidence to demonstrate the controls the entity has placed around ensuring Security Awareness activities are executed and documented as required by the NERC CIP Standards.

Cyber Security Policy Controls

The Controls that must be applied to Security Awareness include:

Control – Conduct Security Awareness on a Scheduled Basis

Security Awareness must be conducted at least once every 15 months.

Recommended Control – Security Awareness Scheduling and Logging

It is recommended that Security Awareness activities be scheduled on a regular basis and assigned to specific people. When a Security Awareness activity is performed, it is also best to log the information at the time, along with supporting evidence. This is the best way to ensure Security Awareness is on track and will go a long way in reducing the number of issues that need to be resolved during the review.

6 – Physical Security Controls

The NERC Standard CIP-003-6 Requirement R2 Section 2 requires registered entities to define and implement Physical Security Controls on their Low Impact BES assets.

The required controls for Low Impact only BES assets must restrict or monitor access to BES assets.

Access controls apply to things like the doors, gates, and check-stations we must pass through to gain access to a BES asset.

Monitoring controls are used for surveillance. These controls use cameras, alarms, and people to watch restricted areas.

Where possible, it is best to use both access and monitoring controls as together, they are far more effective than either one alone. For compliance purposes, though, only one control is required.

To achieve and maintain ongoing compliance, the following actions will need to be taken.

Task 1 – Document Physical Security Controls

Physical Security Controls for Low Impact only BES assets requires the use of one or more access controls. Controls can come in the form of access control and monitoring. These controls can include:

1) Access Controls
   a. Card Key
   b. Locks
   c. Perimeter Controls
2) Monitoring Controls
   a. Camera

    b. Alarm System

    c. Monitored CCTV

    d. Human Observation

The controls that are used for each BES asset must be identified and documented. The example list of controls above can be modified, expanded or adapted as needed by each entity.

Once the controls in use are documented, supporting evidence must be gathered to demonstrate their use. When this is complete, Physical Security Controls are ready for review.

Task 2 – Review Physical Security Controls

Reviewing Physical Security Controls is desirable to ensure all Physical Security Controls have been identified and documented with supporting evidence for each applied control for all BES assets in scope.

While the review is not mandatory (does not directly meet a compliance requirement), it is the best way to be certain the entity has implemented and documented mandatory Physical Security Controls.

For each applied control for each BES asset, the reviewer should confirm that Physical Security Controls are in place and verify that supporting evidence has been collected, and demonstrates compliance

If the Physical Security Controls are not approved, the reviewer needs to document the issues that were uncovered and the work needs to be sent back to the document task (task 1) to resolve the issues.

Compliance Checklist

The optional compliance checklist items that may be considered for this task are:

1) Physical Access Controlled for all BES assets?
2) Evidence verified for all documented Physical Security Controls?

Physical Security Controls – Controls

The Controls that must be applied to Physical Security Controls include:

Control – Require initial assessment
It is required that an initial assessment be performed.

Control – Perform on change to Physical Security Controls
There is no requirement for a periodic review of Physical Security Controls, however, when changes are made these activities should be performed to ensure the entity's Physical Security Controls are in a state of compliance and that the evidence exists to demonstrate it.

Control – Perform the process on a BES asset change
Physical Security Controls should also be reviewed whenever a BES asset is added or removed from the entity's compliance scope to ensure compliance records and evidence are accurate and up-to-date.

7 – Electronic Access Controls

The NERC Standard CIP-003-6 Requirement R2 Sections 3, including subsections 3.1 and 3.2, requires registered entities to define and implement Electronic Access Controls on their Low Impact BES assets.

The first step was to identify the Low Impact BES Assets that have low impact routable connectivity (LERC) and/or dial-up connectivity. That was accomplished during the BES asset Assessment.

Once identified, each Low Impact BES Asset that meets the criteria above must have electronic access controls implemented for its affected BES Cyber Systems and/or Cyber Assets including, at a minimum:

1) permit only necessary inbound and outbound communications and
2) authenticate dial-up connectivity.

As part of documenting electronic access controls, the types of controls used for the low impact routable connectivity and dial-up should be collected along with supporting evidence, demonstrating the implementation of each.

To achieve and maintain ongoing compliance, the following actions will need to be taken.

Task 1 – Document Electronic Access Controls

Electronic Access Controls for Low Impact only BES assets requires the use of one or more inbound and outbound communications controls. Some of the controls that are expected to be used for low impact routable connectivity include:

1) Restricting IP addresses
2) Restricting Ports
3) Restricting Services
4) Deny by Default Firewall Rules

Some of the controls that are expected to be used for authenticating dial-up connectivity are:

1) Preprogrammed number dial out
2) Dial-back modem
3) Remote control modem

The controls that are used to protect the affected BES Cyber Systems and/or Cyber Assets for each BES asset must be identified and documented. The example list of controls above can be modified, expanded or adapted as needed by each entity.

Once the controls in use are documented, supporting evidence must be gathered to demonstrate their use. For example, evidence for "Deny-by-Default" could be demonstrated through a review of deny-by-default electronic access policies and restrictions could be demonstrated through of assessment to ensure all applicable Cyber Assets are within a protected perimeter that applies the appropriate restrictions. When all of the controls and supporting evidence have been collected, Electronic Access Controls are ready for review.

Task 2 – Review Electronic Access Controls

Reviewing Electronic Access Controls is desirable to ensure all Electronic Access Controls have been identified and documented with supporting evidence for each applied control for all BES assets in scope.

While the review is not mandatory (does not directly meet a compliance requirement), it is the best way to be certain the entity has implemented and documented mandatory Electronic Access Controls.

The reviewer should confirm that Electronic Access Controls are in place for the BES Cyber Systems and/or Cyber Assets of each qualifying BES asset, and should also verify that supporting evidence has been collected, and demonstrates compliance, for each applied control.

If the Electronic Access Controls are not approved, the reviewer needs to document the issues the uncovered and the work needs to be sent back to the first task (task 1) to resolve the issues.

Compliance Checklist
The optional compliance checklist items that may be considered for this task are:
  1) Electronic Access Controlled for all BES Assets or BES Cyber System locations?
  2) Supporting Evidence Confirmed for each Outbound Connection Confinement Method Employed?

Electronic Access Controls – Controls

The Controls that must be applied to Electronic Access Controls include:

Control – Require initial assessment
It is required that an initial assessment be performed.

Control – Perform on change to Electronic Access Controls
There is no requirement for a periodic review of Electronic Access Controls, however, when changes are made these activities should be performed to ensure the entity's Electronic Access Controls are in a state of compliance and that the evidence exists to demonstrate it.

Control – Perform the process on a BES asset change
Electronic Access Controls should also be reviewed whenever a BES asset is added or removed from the entity's compliance scope to ensure compliance records and evidence are accurate and up-to-date.

8 – Incident Response Plan

The NERC Standard CIP-003-6 Requirement R2 Section 4, subsections 4.1 – 4.6 requires registered entities to have an Incident Response Plan and to respond to a real Incident or perform a test of the Incident Response Plan at least once every thirty-six (36) months.

Cyber security incidents are detected security-related events that may represent an actual incident. Real incidents require a formal response that can involve a number of activities and people.

An Incident Response plan is needed to provide definition and structure around how the organization will handle things like identifying potential incidents, classifying them and responding to them. To do this, the Incident Response Plan must address how:

1. Potential Incidents are
   a. detected or identified
   b. assessed and classified
2. Real Incidents are
   a. responded to
   b. determined if they are Reportable
3. Reportable Incidents
   a. are reported
4. Incident Response Plan updates are
   a. completed after an Incident or test

It's helpful to also look at things from the perspective of Incidents by breaking them down into their respective stages as follows:

Stage 1	Stage 2	Stage 3
(potential)	(real or not)	(reportable or not)
Undetected	Real	Reportable
Detected	Not Real	Not Reportable

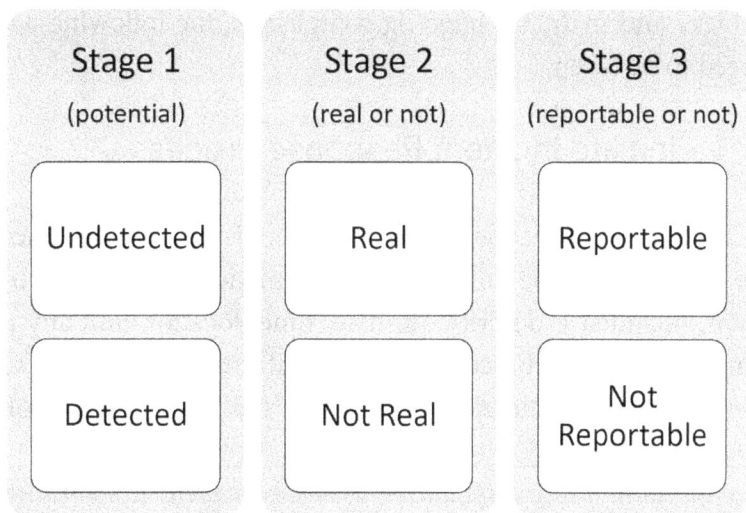

Undetected - Potential Incident (we don't know it exists)

Detected - Potential Incident (we know it exists, but not a lot else)

Non-Incident - (it's been reviewed and determined to not be an Incident)

Real Incident - (it's been reviewed and is a Real Incident)

Real Addressed Incident - (the Incident has been responded to and the response is complete)

Reportable Incident - (the Incident must be reported to E-ISAC)

Roles and Responsibilities

There is also a requirement to have the roles and responsibilities required to perform the Incident Response Plan identified, either by groups or as individuals. This implies the need to maintain this list of Responders, including updating, and then notifying Responders when there are changes to the Incident Response Plan.

These are the people responsible for responding to an Incident and they need to know about any changes to the Plan that might affect how they perform their role in responding to a Cyber Security Incident.

To achieve and maintain ongoing compliance, the following actions will need to be taken.

Task 1 – Initiate Incident Response Process

Every time a potential cyber security incident is detected, the Incident Response Plan must be initiated and information about the potential incident, included a description, date, time, location and any other relevant details must be collected. This information will be used to assess the potential incident to determine if it is a Real Incident or not.

Note – the same process should be used for Incident Response testing so it's important to have a way to indicate if it is a Test (or not) in the initiation task.

Task 2 – Classify the Incident

All potential incidents (and tests) must be classified in order to determine a) is it a Real Incident? b) to perform any additional classification per the entity's Incident Response Plan (that may affect how the organization responds to the Incident).

The personnel responsible for classifying the potential Incident will need the information collected in the Initiate task and may need to perform additional research to determine if the potential Incident is a Real Incident or not. Once that determination is made, it must be recorded. Determining if the Incident is Reportable and documenting it is also likely to be performed in this task. The date the classification is completed should also be recorded.

If the Incident is not a Real Incident (or a test), no further tasks are required.

Task 3 – Respond to the Incident

Once an Incident is classified as a Real Incident, the organization must respond to the Incident based on its Incident Response Plan. As part of this activity, it is important to document the organization's response to the Incident and any lessons learned from the experience of dealing with the Incident.

Compliance Checklist
The optional compliance checklist items that may be considered for this task are:
1) Does the Response Adhere to the Incident Response Plan?
2) Are there are any Lessons Learned from this Incident?

Task 5 – Report Incident

All reportable Incidents must be reported to E-ISAC within 180 calendar days from the completion of the response. During this process, evidence should be collected including:
1) Copy of the information supplied to E-ISAC
2) Evidence that the Incident was Reported (i.e. – copies of communications)
3) Date the Incident was Reported
4) Who the Incident was Reported to
5) Any additional communication between E-ISAC and the entity

Task 6 – Update Incident Response Plan

After each Incident Response and Test, it is required that the entity assess the Incident Response in order to determine if there are any things can be learned from the Incident Response that can be used to improve the plan.

Based on any of these lessons-learned, the Incident Response Plan must be updated to address the lessons-learned.

Compliance Checklist

The optional compliance checklist items that may be considered for this task are:

1. Incident Response Plan Updated?
2. All Lessons-Learned Addressed?
3. Job Role or Responsibility Changes?
   3.1 Roles and Responsibilities updated in Plan?
   3.2 Notifications sent to Responders?

Control – Perform on a Schedule (test)

The Incident Response Plan must be tested at least once every thirty-six (36) months.

Note – if the Plan is activated for a detected potential incident, the response to that resets the 36-month clock.

Control – Perform on Detected Potential Incident

The Incident Response Plan must be activated for each Detected Potential Incident.

9 – Closing Remarks

At times it may seem like a thankless task, ensuring your organization has a solid cyber security baseline and achieving compliance with NERC CIP. As long as the lights keep staying on, most of the world doesn't even notice.

But we do. We know how much effort, energy, and dedication goes into keeping our grid secure from those with mal-intent. We also know that most of the people that are doing that work have a lot of other responsibilities, many standing ahead of compliance responsibilities. Unsung heroes, each and every one.

We hope this book has helped paint a picture for you, one that makes it easier to understand what you need to do, and what to consider when you do so.

Just how important is NERC CIP? Besides punitive measures like fines, there are 300 million other reasons why it's important – the people in this great country of ours. Their work, their comfort, and their very lives depend on us, let's make sure we never leave them in the dark!

About the Authors

TERRY SCHURTER is the President of CIP Core, Inc. (www.cipcore.org), a non-profit corporation focused on providing training resources to regulated entities for BES Reliability, and Controls Strategist for Qualtrax (www.qualtrax.com).

Terry has won awards for controls engineering, software development, and the Global Thought Leadership award from the BPM Group. He served as the Research Director for Process with Bloor Research, and has provided strategic advisement to a range of software clients.

Terry cofounded several startups, including the xFactory (MES) software solution. He developed and delivered process improvement training to companies globally (US, UK, Australia, UAE, Belgium, France, Germany, Switzerland) and was a Keynote Speaker at Fortune 100 C-level conferences. He has worked with multiple public sector clients.

Terry is a published author/co-author including Protecting Critical Infrastructure with Karl Perman, Customer Expectation Management, the Insiders' Guide to BPM, Technologies for Government Transformation, and In Search of BPM Excellence. He has over 30 years' experience managing and implementing solutions for engineering, software, and business problems.

KARL PERMAN is the Senior Vice President of CIP Core, His responsibilities include strategic direction, organizational development and creation of educational content.

In addition to CIP Core, Karl serves the energy sector as a

consultant in the areas of NERC compliance, cybersecurity, physical security, reliability, and risk management and as an educator in criminal justice, security and information technology disciplines including service as a faculty member at the University of Phoenix. He has held critical infrastructure protection leadership positions in the energy sector including Exelon Corporation and Southern California Edison. Karl was also the first Director of Security for the North American Transmission Forum and led the security practices group.

Karl served in law enforcement roles at the municipal and federal levels prior to entering the private sector. He also served in the U.S. Army Reserves.

Karl has a Master's Degree in Public Safety Administration from Lewis University and a Bachelor's Degree in Public Law and Government from Eastern Michigan University.

MARC GRAYSON is President and Founder of Baltira (www.Baltira. com) an independent, multi-specialty regulatory compliance and security resources firm. He assists utility clients in executing their compliance vision into positive results. Associates of his firm become a member of your team, assisting in new or ongoing compliance activities. Baltira assists Registered Entities on both the Critical Infrastructure Protection (CIP) standards and Operations & Planning (O&P) standards.

In addition to Baltira, Marc co-founded CIP Core, Inc. and serves as Senior Vice President of Customer Success. Marc is a risk, audit and compliance professional with extensive experience in power, energy, DoD/military and government sectors. Recently as a regulatory compliance manager at the nation's 3rd largest public power utility, Marc drove NERC CIP V3 to V5 implementation efforts to completion across control centers, transmission stations and generation resources. He achieved "no finding" in prior NERC CIP audits with regional entities and led his organization through a rare FERC audit. Marc brings to CIP Core a personal understanding of the challenges utility customers face, uniquely advocating the "position of the client" in all interactions, ensuring clients ultimately achieve transparent and effective cyber security awareness and regulatory compliance within their organization.

LEARN MORE ABOUT
Protecting Critical Infrastructure

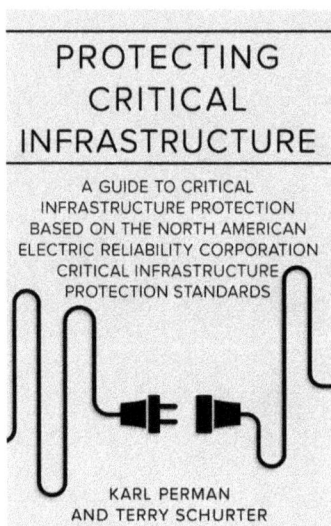

PROTECTING CRITICAL INFRASTRUCTURE

A GUIDE TO CRITICAL
INFRASTRUCTURE PROTECTION
BASED ON THE NORTH AMERICAN
ELECTRIC RELIABILITY CORPORATION
CRITICAL INFRASTRUCTURE
PROTECTION STANDARDS

KARL PERMAN
AND TERRY SCHURTER

... discusses the NERC CIP standards, paying specific attention to the broader implications of the Standards as well as the specific application of the Standards for Regulated Entities that must prove their compliance against NERC CIP.

A must read for anyone with critical infrastructure protection compliance responsibilities. Karl and Terry breakdown the complex NERC CIP requirements into an understandable framework for all levels of utility compliance expertise. If you need to a crash course in NERC CIP compliance, this is it. - Brian Proctor, Utility Cybersecurity expert

Too many of us have been affected by security breaches in our retail, healthcare and financial institutions. But have you thought about power, water, or public transportation? It is vital that our critical infrastructures are protected from both physical and cyber threats. This book provides an excellent path for using a set of current standards (North American Electric Reliability Corporation (NERC) Standards) to inform the security and protection of other critical infrastructures. - Kirsten E. Hoyt, Ed.D. Academic Dean, College of Information Systems and Technology

This book provides an excellent introduction to critical infrastructure protection requirements in the electric utility industry. Highly recommended to anyone new to the market or in need of a refresher. - Michael Trautman, VP & CTO, FoxGuard Solutions

Available at:
Print: http://www.amazon.com/
Protecting-Critical-Infrastructure-Reliability-Corporation/dp/0997252227
eBook: https://ganxy.com/i/112294

www.ingramcontent.com/pod-product-compliance
Lightning Source LLC
Chambersburg PA
CBHW071124210326
41519CB00020B/6406